Hans Christian Andersen

A Fairy Tale Life

by Elizabeth Cote

illustrated by Luciano Lazzarino

Rourke Enterprises   Vero Beach, Florida

Manufactured in the United States of America

Library of Congress Cataloging-in-Publication Data

Cote, Elizabeth, 1957-
  Hans Christian Andersen, a fairy tale life / Elizabeth Cote.
    p. cm. —(Reaching your goal)
  Summary: A biography of the nineteenth century Danish
author whose fairy tales brought him world renown. In-
cludes advice on setting and reaching goals.
    1. Andersen, H.C. (Hans Christian) 1805-1875—
Biography—Juvenile literature. 2. Authors, Danish—19th
century—Biography—Juvenile literature. [1. Andersen,
H.C. (Hans Christian), 1805-1875. 2. Authors, Danish.]
I. Title. II. Series.
PT8119.C68   1989
839.8'136—dc19
[B]   88-16962
[92]   CIP
ISBN 0-86592-430-9   AC

The little boy sat quietly by his father's side. His father read stories from a big book. The stories were full of adventures. The little boy's name was Hans Christian Andersen. Hans loved to listen to stories, and he loved to tell them too.

Hans was born in Denmark, a small country in Europe. The Andersen family was very poor. Their house had one small room and a tiny kitchen. In the small room was his parents' bed and his father's workbench. Hans slept on a rollaway bed.

Hans's parents were hard-working people. His mother did not know how to read or write. His father did, and he even owned a few books. He knew that it was important for Hans to go to school.

Mr. Andersen was a shoemaker. He did not make much money. He didn't want his son to be poor. Mr. Andersen wanted his son to have a better life.

Hans's father spent much of his time with his son. On Sunday afternoons, he took Hans for walks in the woods. Sometimes his father made toys for Hans.

One day Hans and his father went to the theater. Hans loved the pretty costumes, the excitement, and the actors. Hans decided he wanted to be an actor. He wanted to be famous.

Hans begged his father to build him a toy theater. Mr. Andersen built one, and Hans used paper dolls as actors. He sewed costumes for the dolls. He made up stories and plays to act out in his theater.

Hans grew up to be very tall and thin. He had big hands and feet. He often fell over things or bumped into them. He was clumsy.

Hans didn't have many friends. He did not do well in school, because he did not study. Instead, he made up stories. Many children in school teased Hans. They thought he was odd. Because of this, Hans left school. He spent most of his time alone.

When Hans was 11 years old, his father died. Hans missed him very much. He spent more and more time making up stories. Sometimes, people asked to hear a story. Telling stories was the only thing that made Hans happy.

One day Hans decided to put on a play he had written. He invited the neighbors over to watch it. The neighbors were not educated, and they did not understand the play. They thought Hans was wasting his time, and they made fun of him. He should be a shoemaker like his father, they said.

Hans was hurt by his neighbors' unkind remarks. He didn't want to be a shoemaker. "I will be famous!" he shouted to them.

Hans wrote another play. This time, he didn't show the play to his neighbors. He read it to his mother instead. She liked the play but was worried about Hans. She was afraid he would never make much money writing plays.

11

Hans's mother married again. Hans, his mother, and his new stepfather lived in a little house near a river. Hans's family was still poor, so Hans was sent to work in a cloth mill to earn money.

When Hans worked, he sang songs. He also recited plays and told stories. The strong, young workers laughed at Hans. They made fun of his beautiful voice too. He was just too different from them. They could not accept him.

Hans's next job was in a factory. The workers there liked to hear Hans sing and tell stories. Some of the workers told Hans that he was a born actor.

Working in a dirty factory made Hans sick. Hans's mother thought he should become a tailor. Hans's stepfather agreed, but Hans had other ideas. He wanted to be an actor. He knew he had to move to the city of Copenhagen. All the important actors lived in Copenhagen. Denmark's largest theater is there.

When Hans turned 14, he took all the money he had saved and set off for Copenhagen. He was sure that he would become a famous actor.

He found out where some of the famous people lived and introduced himself to one actress. He hoped that she would help him get a part in a play. The actress turned Hans away.

Hans went to the manager of a big theater. The manager told Hans to go home and go back to school. Hans was worried. The money that took him a year to save was almost gone.

Hans Christian Andersen was not ready to give up. He tried singing, but his voice cracked. He tried dancing, but he was too clumsy. He failed at everything he tried.

At 16, Hans was still not famous. He had come to Copenhagen poor, and he was still poor. During the cold, wet winter, he walked around in shoes with holes in the soles. His clothes were almost worn away to rags. He was always hungry, and he had no money to buy food.

One day a friend read a poem Hans had written. Hans's friend liked the poem. This gave Hans the idea of becoming a writer for the theater.

Hans wrote two plays and sent them to a theater director. The director liked Hans's plays, but said they were poorly written. "I think you can become a writer," said the theater director, "but first you must go back to school. You must learn how to spell and write clearly."

Hans went back to elementary school when he was 17! Learning to read and write was hard for Hans. It was even harder for him to sit among boys who were much younger than he was.

Hans thought school would never end. Still, he tried his best. He knew that he had to finish school to become a writer. After five years of hard work, he finally finished elementary school.

Hans began writing poems and books. He wrote some fairy tales for children too. To his surprise, people liked his fairy tales more than his poems and books. Hans wrote "The Emperor's New Clothes," "The Princess and the Pea," "The Little Mermaid," and "The Ugly Duckling."

Many people think that "The Ugly Duckling" tells the story of Hans Christian Andersen's own life. Read the story and see if you agree.

Hans Christian Andersen's fairy tales made him famous. He traveled to many countries. Kings and queens invited Hans to their castles.

"The Little Mermaid" became one of Denmark's favorite fairy tales. A statue of the Little Mermaid sitting on a rock is in Copenhagen harbor. It reminds people that Hans Christian Andersen was a great writer.

Hans Christian Andersen died in 1875. In some ways his life was like a fairy tale, because it had a happy ending. Hans struggled and struggled, and he finally succeeded.

Today, over 100 years later, Hans Christian Andersen is still famous. Children and adults all around the world love his stories.

Reaching Your Goal

What are your goals? Here are some steps to help you reach them.

1. **Decide on your goal.**
   It may be a short-term goal like one of these:
   learning to ride a bike
   getting a good grade on a test
   keeping your room clean
   It may be a long-term goal like one of these:
   learning to read
   learning to play the piano
   becoming a lawyer

2. **Decide if your goal is something you really can do.**
   Do you have the talent you need?
   How can you find out? By trying!
   Will you need special equipment?
   Perhaps you need a piano or ice skates.
   How can you get what you need?
   Ask your teacher or your parents.

3. Decide on the first thing you must do.
Perhaps this will be to take lessons.

4. Decide on the second thing you must do.
Perhaps this will be to practice every day.

5. Start right away.
Stick to your plan until you reach your goal.

6. Keep telling yourself, "I can do it!"

Good Luck! Maybe some day you will become an author like Hans Christian Andersen!

Reaching Your Goal Books

Beverly Cleary She Makes Reading Fun

Bill Cosby Superstar

Jesse Jackson A Rainbow Leader

Ted Kennedy, Jr. A Lifetime of Challenges

Christa McAuliffe Reaching for the Stars

Dale Murphy Baseball's Gentle Giant

Dr. Seuss We Love You

Samantha Smith Young Ambassador

Michael Jordan A Team Player

Steven Spielberg He Makes Great Movies

Charles Schulz Great Cartoonist

Cher Movie Star

Ray Kroc Famous Restaurant Owner

Hans Christian Andersen A Fairy Tale Life

Henry Cisneros A Hard Working Mayor

Jim Henson Creator of the Muppets

Rourke Enterprises, Inc.
P.O. Box 3328
Vero Beach, FL 32964

B
AND

Cote, Elizabeth.

Hans Christian
Andersen, a fairy
tale life.

DATE DUE	BORROWER'S NAME	ROOM NO.
6/19	Terron Robinson	6-30
12/23/92	Denise	5 343

B
AND

Cote, Elizabeth.

Hans Christian
Andersen, a fairy
tale life.

792856 61892D 17276F